Along Love's Pathway

by

Hannah Maynard

Augur Press

ALONG LOVE'S PATHWAY

Copyright © Hannah Maynard 2014

The moral right of the author has been asserted

British Library Cataloguing in Publication Data.
A catalogue record for this book is available from
the British Library.

ISBN 978-0-9571380-5-6

First published 2014 by
Augur Press
Delf House
52 Penicuik Road
Roslin
Midlothian EH25 9LH
United Kingdom

Printed by Lightning Source

Along Love's Pathway

Dedication

For my beautiful daughters, Victoria and Hermione, whose love knows no bounds, and for my man in the moon whose love I will never forget.

Contents

Preface

The author's writing carries in it a simplicity and directness of expression. It has a freshness and honesty which is striking. It is natural, genuine and uncontrived. This is a remarkable achievement considering the complexities inherent in the subject she embraces.

This collection of her work begins with several poems that are a personal examination of what, to her, maturing love actually is. Then follows a series of poems which document the relentless misery that so often has to be endured after the fracturing of an intimate relationship by 'the other'. The effects of being 'dumped' are conveyed very clearly indeed. The reader will note repetitive themes that are characteristic of this kind of raw protracted agony.

As an essential part of the tortuous long drawn out process of achieving emotional separation, the sufferer reaches the depths of despair – a kind of death – a state that is beyond tears. This is expressed very effectively in *Empty vessel*. After dwelling in that state, although in severe emotional pain, she is living again, slowly processing her grief. The poems about this describe rising out of the overwhelming agony of feeling torn apart, to feel a person again, in touch with a sense of self and looking outwards into life.

The sufferer had to endure the pain, *believing that it would never end*. That is what it feels like at the time, and no one ever knows how long it will last.

Introduction

I grew up in a town in South Wales with my parents and my two brothers. I wrote my first poem in primary school when I was ten. I had been the narrator for a school play, and I wrote a poem of the experience. I remember taking it into school the next day and the teacher told me to take it to other classes to read it out.

At secondary school I studied English literature and Law at A level. During this time I saw that same teacher again when I was out shopping in town. He asked me if I was still writing. I smiled and told him that I hadn't written for many years. He said: 'I always remember your writing. Don't stop writing.'

After I left secondary school my parents divorced, so I moved to a small village twelve miles from town. I still live within three miles of that village.

While studying for a secretarial qualification, I supported myself by working as a checkout operator. A year later I met someone, and became pregnant quite soon afterwards. We had two beautiful daughters together, but our relationship broke down and I have raised our children on my own ever since.

I started to write again about four years ago. I was in a very important relationship at the time. I wrote many poems for the person I loved so much, and two of these appear in this book – 'He' and 'He sleeps'. I wrote these with overwhelming love. He always encouraged me to keep on writing, even when the relationship broke down. Since then I have continued to write about how I was feeling, as you will see in many of the poems here.

I write to express feelings that can often be overpowering, and I also write of moments that are so touching that I feel strongly compelled to write. A photograph of such a moment could never do justice to it. To look inside someone's heart and express the depth of emotion felt requires an entirely different modality.

When I write I can often find myself overwhelmed emotionally by the intensity of feeling, and at times I have found myself in tears. It can be at any time that something will pop into my head and I'll have to write it down. It could even be in the middle of the night, mulling over thoughts and emotions, and I'll reach for a pen and paper, letting everything pour out.

Last year, one of my poems – *That Girl* – was published in an anthology called 'One Week Poetry Challenge'. The poem is about seeing a person without actually seeing who they are.

Over the past few years I completed further study, gaining a retail management diploma. During this time, I worked as manager of a charity shop. Due to personal experiences I left that job, and for the past year I have been working as a clerk in a village post office.

I still continue to write as much as I can. Sometimes a compelling force insists that I *must* write! Poetry is what I love to write, but I have started to work on a novel, although this is very much in its infancy. I read a lot of novels, and I also like to bake – mostly cakes. My daughters, now aged 10 and 12 years, seem to enjoy them a lot! In September, they will both be in secondary school.

Hannah Maynard, July 2014

Hello

Writing away on my laptop
A face popped up from the past,
My heart skipped a beat in surprise,
Whatever I did I would have to think fast.

I pondered for a few moments,
Hadn't expected to see him that day,
How I wanted to talk to him,
But, oh, what should I say?

I clicked the icon, stared at the screen,
Knots tightening in my belly.
Don't be ridiculous girl,
He's only human. Don't be silly.

So I typed 'hey', not original by far,
But no words would enter my head.
Wait for a reply… Would I be ignored?
It's the thing we all dread.

A few minutes pass and you fear the worst,
You slink away not making a show.
Just as you're about to shut the screen down,
Up pops the word 'Hello'.

So there is where it all began my friends.
A tale of eternal love and woe,
With such meek and humble beginnings,
That simple word 'Hello'.

'He'

Define being in love.
What does it mean to you?
The smell of honeysuckle in summer sun,
The glimmer of morning dew.
Snowflakes in the winter,
Dancing in the rain,
The scent of wild flowers in the field where you
have lain.
Hope and happiness,
Smiles and laughter,
Plans for the future with a happy ever after.
Hands that hold you tight,
Arms that reach out when you fall,
The kiss that catches your tears,
The one who is there through it all.

The beauty of love becomes bitter in pain,
Sapping strength, erasing hope.
No longer able to dance in the rain.

Pain that separates strength from reason,
Makes you feel irrational, makes you say hurtful
things,
Things you never meant at all.
An all-consuming feeling.

Tears stain tattoo-like on your face.
With a constant ache deep inside,
You mourn that last embrace.

How do you define being in love?
For you, what would it be?
For me the answer is easy…
The definition is 'He'.

He sleeps

He sleeps …
So beautiful, like the moon in a cloudless sky,
Inky blackness darted with brilliant white stars.
The rise and fall of his chest, like waves of the
deepest ocean,
His breath, like the softest breeze rustling
through trees,
Stirring the leaves into a slow dance.
I stop and watch in awe as he gently dreams
away,
Unaware of the pure beauty I see in front of me,
Of the love he fills my heart with,
How he completes my life.
I watch him with pure love in my eyes.
I watch him as …
… He sleeps.

Beside you

Some days I miss you like crazy,
It's a constant ache in my heart.
The days seem long and empty,
I hate that we're apart.

But when I'm feeling lonely,
Feeling sad and blue,
I just think of your love,
I know it will get me through.

Your love is like a blanket,
Wrapped around me tight,
Cosy, soft and warm,
Protecting me through the night.

I look into your eyes,
I see the hurt and sorrow,
But I promise you my darling
I'll help you for every tomorrow.

I'll laugh with you, I'll cry with you,
I'll tightly hold your hand.
You'll never need to feel alone
As beside you is where I stand.

The dream

Waking from slumber
Feel your hand on my face.
Resting contentedly
My outline you trace.
My eyes closed,
Your hand in my hair,
Knowing for certain
It belongs there.
Your tender hand,
A caressing touch,
Feeling complete,
Oh, I've missed you so much.
Arms locked around me,
Your breath on my face,
Feel your heart beating,
A loving embrace.
Feet and legs tangled,
So close we're as one,
Bodies entwined beautifully,
No need to be undone.
The smell of your skin,
Feeling you near,
I turn to face you …

… but you're not even here.

You were never there.

Yet it seemed so real.

I'd wished for you so badly.

It had been just a dream.

Broken

The day you left and said goodbye
Was the day that I started to cry.
The day when everything fell apart
And inky blackness pervaded my heart.
The tears fell, filled with shame
Was it me? Was I to blame?
Did I not love you enough?
Was life with me really that tough?
Did you just stop loving me?
Or are you so scared of what might be?
I know our love is still strong, but now I feel guilty,
As if loving you is wrong.
I tried to fix it but you said no
And now for you it must be so.
I can't pretend my heart didn't break
Or every second I don't feel it ache.
I grieve for the plans we made,
For the dreams that just seem to fade,
For the wedding day when we would both cry,
For our little miracle with her daddy's eyes.

So now I sit in faded light
And make my wishes to the night
Under a moon that lights up both our skies
And the tears that have run from both my eyes.
In all the hurt and sorrow –
The likes I will feel again tomorrow –
I'll never regret us, or meeting this way,
Not even for one single day.
I may get silly and say silly things
But that is what heartbreak brings.

Yet through my greatest love I met my greatest friend
And without you my life would end.

For you

It hurts so much without you,
I have felt my heart break.
An empty shell
without its soul.
I need you with me
to make me whole.
A heart breaking makes a sad soul.
Tears cascading like a waterfall.
You have my heart, you have my soul.
You are my everything, you are my all.
My heart beats for you.
My place is by your side.
My love for you will always be true,
You have filled me with such pride.
Forever I will be yours,
My heart will never stray.
Keep my heart, it is yours.
Never give it away.
It beats for you and you alone,
It hears you call from afar.
It seeks you out when days are done,
Like the bright North star.
The promise of my love
For always is given to you.
I will love you forever more
You can trust my promise is true.

I wish you would come back to me
And stop my heart from aching.
But until that day my darling
It will just continue breaking.

Let go

Lying here I wonder …
I smile as I picture your face,
Trying to go back to that special time,
Back to that happy place.
A place so full of love and warmth,
The memories fill my heart,
A happiness that completed me,
The bitterness that you said to part.
I grieve for the life we should have had,
A life we'd planned together,
The future we'd mapped for our family,
One that meant together forever.
But here I lie next to an empty pillow,
Tears dripping off my nose,
A feeling of dread and loneliness
The type only the heartbroken knows.
Our plans all seem to fade away
For you to share with someone new.
I'd believed everything you said to me,
That our love was true.
You say that it's all over,
That I should let you go,
But I'm still here, still in 'our' place,
So how can I do so?

Stay

I think of you when days are long.
I think of you every day you're gone.
Wondering what you're doing now …
Do you wonder about me, some day, somehow?
Do you miss me as I miss you?
Is your heart also breaking in two?
When the moon is in the sky do you miss me there,
To hold tight, run your fingers through my hair?
The silly things that made us laugh.
With you, I'd never felt so daft.
But now this house is an empty place,
With constant tear stains on my face.
I wonder if you'll ever come home,
Or are you always going to roam?
I miss you so much every day.
Please come home, and this time …

Stay!

Empty vessel

A vessel, discarded, empty,
Devoid of hope, devoid of zest.
Once overflowing with life and love,
Now barren.
Broken,
Full of pain.
A deep chasm
Vast,
Dark,
Unforgiving.
Reaching into infinity.
The smiles and joy of yesterday seem so far in the past.
Stretching ahead…
Never reaching the light.
Perpetual gloom.
Unchecked words extinguished the flame within
A labyrinth of unhappiness, with its probing fingers that
spread around,
Engulfing the soul.
Leaving only bitterness.
Coldness.
The empty vessel that never again will be filled.

One day

You never loved me, that much is true.
Now I'm questioning 'Did I ever know you?'
You promised me the world then took it away,
Leaving me to fight through every single day.
You left me with a stranger here
You took away the man I held so dear.
What I'm left with I don't recognise
You suddenly changed, right before my eyes.
You don't understand what you have done
How affected I am by you being gone.
I've never been in love like this before,
But then you went and slammed the door.
I am lost, lonely and in fear
That's how I feel when you aren't near.
You told me 'Stop trying', so I did, for you
But it's not what I wanted, that much you knew.
You think it doesn't hurt me to see you flirt
To see you treat me as nothing more than dirt.
I was the girl who was your world
Now I'm reduced, as nothing.
I *am* nothing, irrelevant, it's how I feel
You can't blame me, it's how you've made it seem.
I guess you helped me live a lie
Now I know all I can do is cry
As here I stand, rooted to the spot
Where, nine months ago, you threw in the lot.
I lost my heart that very day
And I can't get it back, not any way.

I wish you could look me in the eye
So you can see what you've done, how you've made me cry.
You won't even listen, won't even try
You just kept on walking when you said goodbye.
You'll wish you hadn't walked away.
You'll feel gutted when you think of that day.
One day you will see how good you were with me
One day I promise you, you'll see.

Reminisce

So much time has passed,
Still you are gone.
I still miss you,
What could I have done?
My birthday arrived,
I thought you would know.
Maybe you do
But you'd rather not show.
'It's not you, it's me'
That old cliché
Didn't make it easy,
Didn't help me that day.
Off you went
With a 'move on with your life'.
Here I am.
It's still causing me strife.
I don't understand it.
Maybe I'm not the girl you used to know.
Yes, I've changed.
Maybe you *are* that shallow.
I wish you could see me
My heart in my hands,
The way things are now
It's not as we planned.

Where are you now?
Do you miss me at all?
Do you think of me sometimes?
How I wish you hadn't let me fall.
Seems you've disappeared.
Maybe there's another.
I still remember that day clearly
When we promised there'd be no others.
Now I guess I'm history
Just a chapter in your past
Where did the happiness go?
And the love we said would last?
I miss your little messages,
The way you made me smile,
For now I'll sit in sorrow
And reminisce for a while.

Sealed with a kiss and my tears

Sitting alone the day has passed
Your hopes and dreams fading fast.
The life that was once yours for the taking
Now you feel as if life were faking.
Left alone in pain and sorrow
Never wanting another tomorrow.
All you feel now is the pain in your heart
And the empty promises that you will never part.
The love, the fun, the jokes and laughter,
The fairytale and happy ever after
Dreaming of that special dance
But it was taken away with barely a glance.
Left in confusion, utter despair,
Wishing he was here instead of there.
Feeling as if you can't do anything right,
He just wishes you were out of his sight.
The love you see slowly slipping away
And you dread how much love is lost every day.
But you will never be the perfection he sees in his eyes
Keeping you company at night are only your cries.
His arms won't be there to hold you tight
Keeping you safe and warm through the night.
Your head won't rest upon his chest bare
You won't feel his heart beating there.
Forever I will sit and wait
And pray his love never turns to hate.
But tonight I won't see love in his eyes,
Tonight all I will do is cry.

I wrote this poem just for you
So you will always know my love is true.
But wrapped up in it are my fears,
And it is sealed with a kiss and my tears.

The last goodbye

I'll call to you when time is old,
That is when my story will be told.
When my soul is bared,
I'll say things I never dared.
I'll show you the darkness, the secrets I've kept for years,
I'll show you the truth behind all of my fears.
The thousand pieces of my heart
That shattered with true love's depart.
Small talk of the life we lost,
Where distance and stubbornness bore a heavy cost.
Reveal the scars I've had to hide,
With the pain I kept locked inside.
Wrong choices, seen when it's too late,
Call it destiny, maybe fate.
Time should not be left to slip away,
It's precious, every single day.
I'll look to you and hold your hand
And finally you'll understand.
Time doesn't stand still. I start to cry
As we both whisper our last goodbye.

Until I die

The chance is ours for the taking,
This dream is ours for the making.
It's my heart that you're breaking.
Was it our love you were faking?
Was it our hopes you threw away?
Or was it only me who broke that day?
You know I'd be right there. Just say,
And I'd be there for you in every way.
Where is the life that we shared?
I don't even know if you truly cared.
It seems that your heart was spared
And my soul is broken and bared.
I don't know what to do any more,
It's shaken me down to the core.
I pray you walk back through this door,
I always said I loved you more.
Every single day I cry.
All I keep asking is 'why?'
I wish you would just try,
But I know I'll love you until I die.

Too many

Too many days I've waited
Too many tears I've cried
Too many sleepless nights I've lain here
Waiting for you to be by my side.
Too little an effort you made
Too many promises you broke
Too many times you lied
And left me here to choke.
I can't seem to shake it
I can't just say goodbye
I can't forget it happened
All I can do is cry.

Pen, Paper and I

I sit and I write,
It's how I'll climb out of the hole.
I'll get all my feelings on to paper,
That is my goal.
Again I'll be me
And be rid of the pain.
I will become the girl
Who learned to dance in the rain.
I'll open my soul
And pour out my heart.
My writing will soothe me
It will all play a part.
I brace myself to start
And let out a sigh,
Together we'll heal the darkness,
Pen, Paper and I.

The lake

Memories of times
You spent here before
Send up a shiver
On this sun-beaten shore.
Feel of your hand
Wrapped around mine,
So completed, so needed,
A feeling divine.
Young lovers giggling,
They don't even know,
How in just a second
That feeling could go.
Bittersweet memories
As you watch them there,
Remembering times of togetherness
Without a care.
Walking, you see
The world didn't stop there.
No one else noticed
Your life stripped bare.

You look over and see the man,
Looking sad and lost.
How is he feeling?
How much of his life has it cost?
Whilst you sit on that bench
He's looking over at you,
Asking the same questions
That you are asking too.

You look up and smile
To say I hope you're okay,
A secret handshake that says
We're here to fight another day.
Hear the children playing, laughing,
You guess this is the start.
As you leave the lake that day
There's a glimmer of hope in your heart.

A new chapter

A new breath of life
Exhale the old
Hope of a new story
With chapters untold.
Waves crashing forth
Following a cowardly retreat
The warm breeze in your hair
The soft sand under feet.
Give up your trouble
Unto the wind
A place with you, again
they will never find.
This is your haven
Your secret place
Your own little island
Your own special place.
The secrets all left there
To feel free again,
Free of the hurt
Free of the pain.
As you leave your haven
Your breath you hold
As you begin your new story
With its chapters untold.

For other titles from Augur Press
please visit

www.augurpress.com